GROUNDHOG DAY!

BY GAIL GIBBONS

Holiday House / *New York*

FEBRUARY 2

To Eileen Kern

Special thanks to
Bill Deeley, Phil's handler,
Punxsutawny, Pennsylvania,
and John Serrao, professional
naturalist, Tobyhanna,
Pennsylvania

Copyright © 2007 by Gail Gibbons
All Rights Reserved
Printed and bound in April 2019 at
Toppan Leefung. DongGuang City. China.
www.holidayhouse.com
9   10

Library of Congress Cataloging-in-Publication Data
Gibbons. Gail.
Groundhog Day! / by Gail Gibbons. — 1st ed.
p. cm.
ISBN-13: 978-0-8234-2003-2 (hardcover)
ISBN-10: 0-8234-2003-5 (hardcover)
1. Groundhog Day—Juvenile literature. I. Title.
GT4995.G6G53 2007
394.261—dc22
2006003456
ISBN-13: 978-0-8234-2116-9 (pbk)

Groundhog Day is celebrated on February 2. Some people believe that on this day of the year, watching groundhogs can help predict when spring will come.

When will spring begin? The date of February 2 is about the middle of the winter. Old stories say that if a groundhog sees its shadow on this date, there will be about six more weeks of winter.

Those stories also say that if a groundhog doesn't see its shadow, spring will come early.

Groundhog Day grew out of old customs and beliefs. Some ancient peoples celebrated a spring festival in early February. Many people cleaned their houses and the area where they lived, getting ready for a new beginning, the new spring season.

Then about 1,500 years ago, people in Europe began lighting candles in the early spring for a new religious celebration. This practice coincided with the older observances that celebrated the end of winter and the beginning of spring.

To HIBERNATE means to rest and sleep during the winter.

People had always thought that they could predict when spring would come by watching animals. They believed that if a hibernating animal awoke from its sleep in the beginning of February and saw its shadow, there would be several more weeks of winter.

HEDGEHOG

BEAR

BADGER

If the animal didn't see its shadow, spring would come soon.
They watched animals such as hedgehogs, bears, and badgers.

When Europeans were coming to North America, some settled in Pennsylvania. They brought with them the tradition of predicting spring by watching animals.

Many groundhogs lived in this region. Groundhogs are animals that hibernate. It seemed logical to choose groundhogs to predict when spring would arrive.

Early in February people watched groundhogs to find out whether they did or didn't see their shadows. This custom became a yearly celebration in many places, including the town of Punxsutawney (punk·suh·TAW·nee), Pennsylvania.

Then in 1886, Clymer Freas wrote in the town newspaper that February 2 would be called Groundhog Day.

In Punxsutawney the special groundhog is always called Punxsutawney Phil. There have been many Punxsutawney Phils. Every year on February 2 thousands of people show up at Gobbler's Knob just outside of Punxsutawney to find out if Phil will see his shadow.

High up on a stage, Phil is kept in a burrow under a fake tree stump. Town officials are also up on the stage. At exactly 7:25 a.m. Phil is taken out of his burrow. Everyone cheers.

If Phil sees his shadow, winter will be longer. If he doesn't see his shadow, spring will come sooner. The officials make it look as if Phil whispers to one of them whether or not he has seen his shadow. It's all pretend.

Sometimes Phil is right. Other times he is wrong. Lots of people think Groundhog Day is fun.

A GROUNDHOG is also called a WOODCHUCK.

A groundhog is a furry rodent. It is a mammal that can weigh between 5 and 10 pounds (2.3 and 4.5 kg). It usually grows to about 20 inches (50.8 cm) long and has a short tail and short legs. Many people think a groundhog is cute when it waddles around.

18

A GROUNDHOG'S SKULL

INCISOR TEETH

Like other rodents such as mice, squirrels, and beavers, groundhogs have large front teeth that grow continuously. To help wear them down, groundhogs gnaw on, bite, and eat twigs and branches. Their diet also includes leaves, flowers, and berries.

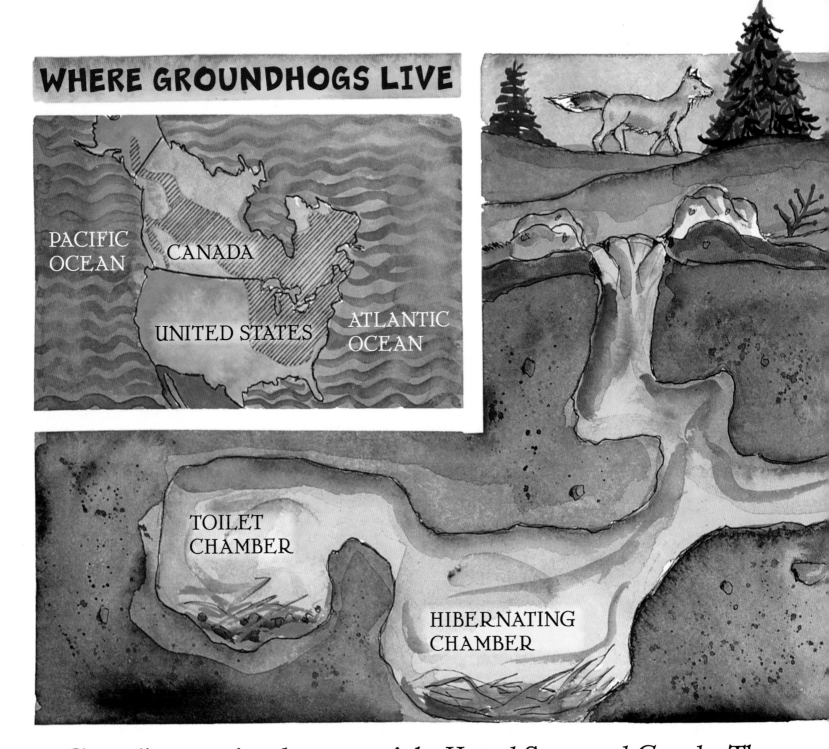

WHERE GROUNDHOGS LIVE

PACIFIC OCEAN

CANADA

UNITED STATES

ATLANTIC OCEAN

TOILET CHAMBER

HIBERNATING CHAMBER

Groundhogs are found in parts of the United States and Canada. They live alone in burrows that they dig out with their sharp, curved front claws. Some burrows can be as deep as 6 feet (1.8 m) and spread out more than 30 feet (9.1 m).

20

NESTING CHAMBER

FOOD STORAGE CHAMBER

SLEEPING CHAMBER

Since they are prey to many animals, groundhogs stay close to home, usually near one of the entrances to their burrows. When outside their burrows, they may sit up straight with their front paws held tightly against their chests, eating and watching for any signs of danger.

When danger is near, groundhogs make a sharp, high-pitched whistle to warn other groundhogs. Some of their natural enemies are wolves, foxes, and birds such as hawks.

22

During the summer groundhogs eat as much as they can to
increase their body fat. In the fall they go into their burrows
to hibernate through the cold winter months. Throughout the
winter their fat provides nourishment to keep them alive.
To save energy, their body temperature drops and their
breathing and heart rate slow down.

There are usually four or five KITS, also called CUBS, in a litter.

In some parts of the United States and Canada, groundhogs poke their tiny noses out of their burrows during February, about the middle of winter. Male groundhogs look for female groundhogs around this time, and they mate. About thirty days later the females give birth to their litters of tiny, blind kits. In the northern areas, all this happens much later.

24

For the first month, the mother groundhogs take very good care of their young. When the kits are about one month old, they open their eyes and begin to crawl about.

When the young groundhogs are about two months old, they are able to leave their mothers to dig their own burrows. A new generation of groundhogs is ready to care for itself.

People enjoy Groundhog Day. Sometimes children draw pictures of groundhogs, have snacks, and play games, such as Shadow Tag.

People read stories to children about Groundhog Day.

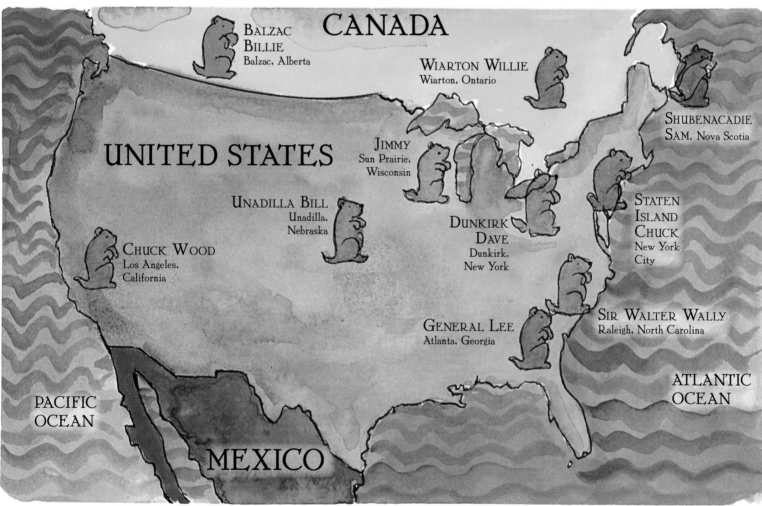

Punxsutawney Phil is the big star. People wait to find out whether or not Phil will see his shadow. There are other famous groundhogs too.

Often gardeners and farmers think groundhogs are pests because they eat their vegetables. Other people think groundhogs are good at tilling the soil when they dig burrows.

Even though groundhogs are not native to every region,
people all over the United States and Canada celebrate
Groundhog Day.

DIGGING UP GROUNDHOG FACTS

When a groundhog hibernates, its teeth stop growing and it takes only one breath about every five minutes.

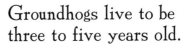

Groundhogs live to be three to five years old.

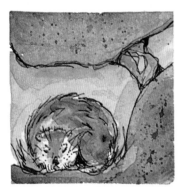

A groundhog's hibernating chamber is the deepest one in the burrow. Often a groundhog plugs up the entrance to this chamber to keep out cold air.

The people who live in Punxsutawney say their town is known as the Weather Capital of the World.

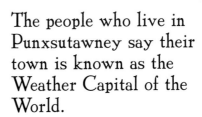

About 700 pounds (317.5 kg) of dirt can be removed by a groundhog digging a very big burrow. Sometimes a groundhog can do this in one day!

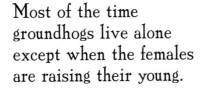

Most of the time groundhogs live alone except when the females are raising their young.

On Groundhog Day people read and listen to the news to find out if spring will come early.

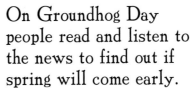